A TALE OF TWO
BEEHIVES

A TALE OF TWO BEEHIVES

Leveraging the Power of Engagement and Working Culture

DR SHAROQ ALMALKI

ARCHWAY
PUBLISHING

Archway Publishing books may be ordered through booksellers or by contacting:

Archway Publishing
1663 Liberty Drive
Bloomington, IN 47403
www.archwaypublishing.com
1 (888) 242-5904

Because of the dynamic nature of the Internet, any web addresses or links contained in this book may have changed since publication and may no longer be valid. The views expressed in this work are solely those of the author and do not necessarily reflect the views of the publisher, and the publisher hereby disclaims any responsibility for them.

ISBN: 978-1-4808-3036-3 (sc)
ISBN: 978-1-4808-3037-0 (hc)
ISBN: 978-1-4808-3038-7 (e)

Library of Congress Control Number: 2016906708

Print information available on the last page.

Archway Publishing rev. date: 09/09/2016

To Faisal and Abrar, who are the real spirit of my motivation.
To my friends who encouraged me.
To all leaders and colleagues who continue
inspiring me for further innovation.
To the leaders of tomorrow.

INTRODUCTION

ONE MORNING, THE OWNER OF A BIG COMPANY woke up to the realization that something was wrong. Sales were down. Profits were stagnant. Employee turnover was high. Some of his best people had left the company to go work for his competitors. From every office and cubicle, he could feel a sense of malaise.

The owner immediately called a business consultant. "You've got to help me," he said. "The company is not doing as well as it should, and I can't figure out why. Please come and make a study. Find out what's wrong."

The consultant came to the company and spent many hours touring the offices and meeting with employees.

"Well, what did you discover?" asked the owner. "Why are we in a slump?"

"You have very poor employee engagement," said the consultant.

"Employee engagement?" replied the owner. "What are you talking about? We pay competitive wages!"

"Wages are important," said the consultant, "but people don't just work for money. They work for satisfaction and for fulfillment. They work to have fun, to learn, and to be recognized. They work for many reasons besides money."

"I still don't understand," said the owner. "In this company, we do things the way they've always been done."

"That's precisely the problem," answered the consultant. She handed a slender book to the owner. "I want you to read this. It will introduce you to employee engagement. The book is called *A Tale of Two Beehives.*"

"Beehives?" said the owner. "Are you kidding?"

"No, I'm not kidding," said the consultant. "It's a fable—a story about an industrious bee named Adam. He works at a beehive very much like this company. He's not happy, but he's loyal to his company. One day, he gets blown off course and lands at a competing hive. There, he sees for himself what a culture of employee engagement can do. The competing hive is profitable, and the bees who work there are happy to be on the job. They're all part of a team, working for a common goal. Adam is amazed! With his newfound insights, he hurries back to his own hive to spread the good news!"

"Yes?" asked the owner. "Then what? Does his hive listen to him? Do they change?"

The consultant smiled. "You'll have to find out for yourself," she said.

The owner took the book. "You want me to read a story about bees?" he asked.

"Yes," replied the consultant. "There's a reason. The book is both informative and a pleasure to read. It's good for you without being dull and boring. It tells you things you need to know without lecturing."

"Let me guess," said the owner. "It's just like employee engagement. It gets positive results and makes you feel good too!"

"Yes," she said. "Enjoy the book. After you've read it, we'll talk about what you can do to improve employee engagement at your company."

"And increase profits?" asked the owner.

"One thing leads to another," she answered. "One thing leads to another."

The owner thanked the consultant and promised to read the book.

You can read it too.

And now, the story of Adam and the two beehives.

Cast of Characters

Queen Minerva's Hive

Adam: a drone who is a traveling salesbee

Susan: a worker in the queen's nursery

James: the befuddled weatherman

Tony: manager of drone activities and Adam's immediate superior

Daria: operations director and member of the queen's executive committee

Ken: a severely disengaged worker

Eva: the inventory manager

John: a novice salesbee

Queen Venus's Hive

Mike: a traveling salesbee, formerly of the Minerva hive
Nancy: a member of the inventory-control team
Robert: the director of human resources
Sara: the marketing bee in charge of social media
Andrew: the supervisor of Mike's sales group
Rachel: a member of the honey-production department

CHAPTER 1

THE HIVE OF QUEEN MINERVA

AS THE FIRST GLIMMER OF DAWN BROKE OVER THE farm, Adam roused himself from his slumber. It was time to go to work.

He emerged from his cubicle and joined the hundreds of other bees who crowded the narrow corridors of the hive, all hurrying and jostling as they went to their appointed stations. At that early hour, no one was in a very good mood, so Adam did his best to avoid personal interaction.

Then he saw Susan, who worked in the queen's nursery. She was one of the few bees who were always cheerful.

He went to her to say hello. It was nice to find someone in the hive in the morning who was not grumpy. "I hope the weather is good today," he said. "I hate flying in the rain or when it's too hot. I like it best when the air is cool and dry."

"I agree," said Susan. "Has James given out the weather forecast?"

Adam shrugged. "You know James. He acts like his information is top secret.

Isn't the weather report vital to our mission? Don't we all need to know what we're going to encounter when we fly to distant places? I don't understand why he isn't more

communicative. Last week, we got caught in a sandstorm and a bunch of us almost didn't make it back by sunset. And you know how much we hate flying at night."

Susan shuddered. "I don't even want to think about it. But you know how it is around here. That's just the way things are. James does what he wants. No one can tell him otherwise. I've gotten used to it so much that I don't even think about it anymore." She looked at her watch. (Yes, these bees wore tiny watches.) "We'd better get going, or we'll be late for the staff meeting."

Adam and Susan joined the line of other bees headed to the meeting room. In a few minutes, the space was crowded. *Too* crowded, in fact.

"I wish they'd make this place bigger," whispered Susan. "Don't they know how difficult it is to hear anything when we're all crammed in here wing-to-wing? You can't even think."

"You'd better keep it down," said a drone in the row behind them.

"Oh, good morning, Ken," said Susan.

Ken grunted. "If you say so. Anyway, you'd better watch what you say. Daria doesn't like complainers. She wants everyone to be happy."

Adam eyed the crowded room. He didn't see Daria, who as the hive's director of operations, reported directly to Queen Minerva. Daria was known for her ability to flatter the queen. She told the queen only good news so that the queen would think Daria was doing a good job.

Adam thought for a moment about Queen Minerva. She ran the hive with an iron fist, but not directly. She always gave her orders through her executive committee, including Daria. In fact, in his entire life, Adam had seen Queen Minerva only once. That was when the queen had conducted an inspection tour of the combs where the honey was stored. Daria had ordered Adam and some other drones to stand at attention—as if they were in the army!—while the queen was carried past. Putting on a show for the queen seemed pointless and silly to Adam, and disappointing. He really wanted to be loyal to his queen and do a good job for her, but it was difficult to get inspired to excel when he barely even knew what Queen Minerva *looked* like. For a lowly drone like Adam, getting to see the queen in person was almost unthinkable. To actually *talk* to the queen? Impossible. A camel could fly before such a thing would happen.

A drone was a drone, and the chain of command was very clear. As part of his job description, Adam reported to his immediate superior, the manager of drone activities, a tough old bee named Tony. As a drone, Adam was not expected to interact with anyone else, especially bees not in his department.

Tony always said, "Talk to other bees? What's the point? You're the expert in your department, and they're the experts in theirs. There is no need to talk to anyone else. It would not do any good. Just do your job and let the other bees do theirs."

Finally, the meeting began—ten minutes late.

"I don't understand how they expect us to get our jobs done when the managers can't even get to the morning meeting on time," Adam whispered to Susan.

In the row behind him, Ken overheard Adam. He chose to say nothing. It was better for him, he thought, if he quietly catalogued expressions of disloyalty made by other bees, whom he viewed not as colleagues but as competitors. After all, he reasoned, there were only a few opportunities for advancement in "the Minerva hive," as they called it. Why should he help any of his colleagues? It was every bee for himself. If he had information that could thwart Adam's progress up the ladder, so much the better.

"Your attention, please!" called a bee from the front of the room.

Adam peered over the heads of the other bees. "It's Tony," he said to Susan. "He's probably going to hand out our assignments."

"Okay, people, listen up!" said Tony. In his tiny hands, he held an old-fashioned clipboard and a pencil. Digital-network technology had not yet arrived at the Minerva hive; the queen thought it was unnecessary. In one of her memos, she had written that they had been making honey the same way for centuries, so why change? Digital upgrades were a needless expense.

"Here are today's assignments," began Tony.

After reading off some other names, he came to Adam. "Let's see," said Tony. "Adam, you are to fly to the bed of caper plants in the eastern end of the green valley. Your quota today is to collect ten drops of nectar."

Adam's hand shot up like a schoolboy's. "Excuse me, Tony, perhaps you've forgotten that just yesterday a team scoured that area and found only five drops among them. I think that—"

Tony glared at Adam. "That will be quite enough, thank you. These plans have been made by the queen's executive council. The assignments we give are based on what has been collected in the past."

"But the man who owns the garden has dug up half the beds," said Adam. "There just aren't as many flowers now as there were last year."

Now Tony was getting angry. "We don't need excuses, Adam. We need results. Just go out and do your job. Unless, of course, you'd like to work at some other hive."

At those words, a hush fell over the room.

Queen Minerva's workers believed that to be kicked out of your hive was a terrible thing. Stories abounded about the bad conditions at other hives. All the stories came from the queen via her memos, but since most bees had never lived in another hive, they accepted what she told them.

"Well, Adam?" said Tony.

"Of course, sir," answered Adam. "No problem. To the caper beds I'll go."

CHAPTER 2

ADAM'S ASSIGNMENT

WHEN ADAM SAID THAT HE'D GO TO THE CAPER beds, everyone in the room breathed a sigh of relief. No one wanted a conflict.

No one, that is, except Ken, who had been secretly hoping that Adam would get into trouble. He was disappointed that Adam had been agreeable.

"Good," said Tony. "Let's have no more nonsense. Now then, James will give the weather forecast."

For the bees who journeyed far from the hive in search of nectar, the weather forecast was extremely important. They listened intently as James began.

"Um, let's see …" James shuffled some tiny papers. "Oh yes, here we are. The valley weather. Oh, sorry. That's yesterday's report. Hang on a second."

Susan leaned close to Adam. "Day after day, it's like this," she whispered. "I like James well enough, but he should have retired years ago. He just can't keep up."

Adam nodded. "I don't think he understands how important this is. And anyway, if this hive had a better pension plan, maybe James wouldn't have to keep working. It seems to me that he's put in enough time and ought to be able to enjoy a nice retirement."

Adam sensed that Ken was leaning forward, as if he were trying to listen to what Adam was saying. Adam shot him a glance, and Ken pretended to casually relax.

"Okay," James continued after shuffling more papers, "the weather in the green valley should be fine. No problems. Everything will be fine."

"Did everyone hear that?" interjected Tony. "The weather will be fine. We expect everyone to go out and put in a full day. Don't come back early unless you've got a full load of nectar."

"Aren't we at the start of the sandstorm season?" asked a bee in another row. "Are you sure that the weather will be clear?"

"You heard what James said," replied Tony. "No excuses. We want results, not complaints. And now, before we break up, the operations manager will give the honey-production report."

Daria stood before the attentive group. The production report was key because it was tied to the workers' benefits.

"People, as you know, we've been having quality-control issues," she said. "In fact, our honey has been downgraded. Years ago, we sold our honey to the finest gourmet shops in the region. Our honey was of the best purity, and no other was sweeter. Unfortunately, that market has dried up. We now sell our product primarily to companies that use it as a flavoring in processed foods. Of course, the price per pound is lower. Food conglomerates don't need the best product. All they want is something they can call 'real honey' that won't poison the consumer. That's our current market."

"What does that mean for us?" asked a drone.

"It means no raises this year," replied Daria. "Sorry, but we need to cut expenses to match our reduced income."

"Why can't we improve our quality to what it used to be?" asked Susan.

"That's a very complicated issue," said Daria. "The executive team is working on it now. When they're ready, they will issue their report."

"*Report*?" whispered Adam to Susan. "We don't need a *report*. Everyone knows that the honey factory hasn't been overhauled in years. We're using equipment that should have been taken to the junkyard long ago. Of course our honey is second-rate. We don't invest in it."

"Adam, do you have something to say?" questioned Daria loudly.

Adam looked at Daria. All the bees in the room looked at Adam. Would he say something or keep his mouth shut?

Adam thought, *What difference will it make? The hive is highly organized, and the queen and her executive team make all the decisions. They know what's best. By speaking up, all I will get is a big headache.*

"Um, no," said Adam. "I have nothing to say."

"Okay, then," said Daria. "Meeting dismissed. Everyone get to work."

"Another day, another flower," said Adam to Susan. "I'll see you later."

Susan nodded. She was headed to her place in the nursery. She had always wanted to be a flier like Adam, but the queen's executive committee handed out the job assignments. There wasn't much you could do to change what they told you. "For the good of the hive," is what they said. They had assigned her to the nursery, and that was that.

Adam headed toward the door, but a line of worker bees blocked the path.

"What's going on?" he asked a bee next to him. "I've got to get out of here. I need to fly all the way to the eastern valley. I'm going to be behind schedule."

The bee shrugged. "Queen Minerva is coming down the corridor. Her guards have the area closed off. No one gets in or out until after she passes."

Adam glanced at his tiny watch. The minutes were ticking by. He pushed his way forward. In front of him stood one of the queen's guards. Adam tapped the guard on the shoulder. "Excuse me," he said. "I've really got to get through. I need to fly all the way to the eastern valley today."

"Sorry," said the guard. "No one passes. You'll have to wait."

Just then, a line of sharply dressed executive bees came along the corridor.

Adam peered over the shoulder of the guard, and he caught a glimpse of Queen Minerva herself. Her expensive outfit was richly decorated with sparkling jewels. The queen stared straight ahead as she was carried along the corridor.

As quickly as she had appeared, she was gone.

Wow, thought Adam. *Daria told us that business was terrible and that we wouldn't be getting raises this year because we needed to cut expenses. I guess no one told the queen. She looks like she's doing very well! If she sold some of those jewels, she could invest in new equipment for the honey factory.*

No matter. Adam had a job to do. As soon as the way was clear, he made his way to the door to the outside world. He was about to take off when he heard a shout from behind. He stopped and turned around.

Tony was right behind him. "Adam," he said as he waved a stack of papers, "there's been a change of plan. You are to fly to a patch of blooming hyacinth plants on the western side of the green valley. Your quota is eight drops of nectar. Okay? Now get going." He turned to hurry away.

"Wait!" called Adam.

Tony stopped. "Yes, what is it?"

"I've never been to the western side of the green valley!" said Adam. "I really don't think that I'm confident about the navigation. What if there are clouds and I cannot see the sun?"

"You'll be fine," replied Tony. "According to James, the weather will be clear. It's a routine flight. Other bees have done it. Now are you just going to stand there or get going? The sun is rising higher by the minute."

What could Adam say? He didn't want to lose his job, or worse, get kicked out of the hive. He had no choice. With a sigh, he turned and headed for the door.

CHAPTER 3

ADAM GETS THE JOB DONE

JAMES, AT LEAST, HAD BEEN CORRECT ABOUT IT being a beautiful, clear day.

Adam took flight and, after getting his bearings by circling the big boxy hive that the farmer had built, headed in the direction of the green valley.

His route to the green valley was familiar: past the farmhouse, over a stand of scrubby trees, then along the old riverbed until he came to a low ridge. On the other side of the ridge was the green valley.

As he flew, he tried to keep his mind on his mission, but too many thoughts kept intruding. Mostly they were thoughts about the way business was conducted at the Minerva hive. Adam didn't have any management experience—for drones like him, such training was not considered to be of any value—but he had a vague sense that things could be better. A lot better.

Many questions swirled through his mind.

Did Queen Minerva really have to be so remote?

How could the executive committee make plans despite the fact that none of them ever left the hive and flew around in the real world?

Why was the decline in sales revenue not a matter of the utmost urgency? Wasn't it obvious that the outmoded equipment in the honey factory was a big problem?

Couldn't information about critical things like the weather be instantly available to everyone who needed to know?

Adam felt a little bit depressed because he knew that the nectar he collected was the very best available. He went to only the freshest flowers, and he always flew a little bit farther to find blossoms that hadn't been picked over by bees from other hives. If you got to a blossom after other bees had been there, there was nothing left but second-rate nectar. That's another reason why Adam tried to leave the hive promptly each morning. He wanted to get a jump on the competition.

He glanced at the sun over his shoulder. It was getting higher in the sky. Adam increased his speed. He'd be tired when he arrived at the valley, but if he had any hope of collecting his quota, he needed to pick up the pace.

Darn that Tony, he thought. *If this project had been planned with more care, I'd be there by now.*

He pushed these negative thoughts out of his head. Adam

always tried to keep a positive attitude. Getting upset, he knew, never gets you anywhere.

Crossing the ridge, he saw the green valley unfold in front of him. It was a lovely place, full of gardens and streams whose cool waters glinted in the sunlight. The way to the east was easy; he had gone there dozens of times. But today he turned west, into unfamiliar territory. He was supposed to fly around a tall building—yes, that must be the one directly ahead. Once past the tall building, he made a slight turn to the north. The garden was long, narrow, and carefully designed. There were red maple trees and a bed of roses. A person was digging in one of the flower beds, probably taking out what they called "weeds." That was something that humans did—they ripped up perfectly good flowering plants. In Adam's mind, a plant either bore blossoms or it didn't. If it did, it was useful. If it didn't, it wasn't useful. Simple as that.

He arrived at the hyacinths. They looked good, but just as he had feared, busy among the blossoms were swarms of insects of many varieties—bees, houseflies, hoverflies, tiny stingless wasps, ants, butterflies, and beetles. Everyone wanted a part of the action.

It was a highly competitive marketplace.

Adam was not deterred. He quickly flew to an isolated plant and got busy among the more obscure blossoms. It did not take long before he had collected ten drops of nectar—two more than his quota. It was good stuff too—not the leftovers that had been picked over by everyone else.

Adam was a very good collector of nectar. In fact, he was regularly a top producer at the Minerva hive. Every January, he had a performance review with Tony. On the appointed day, he would go to Tony's cubicle to meet with his boss. Tony would pore over the field reports and make comments. "Ah, yes," Tony said during Adam's last performance review. "Let's see … during the last two quarters, you were number one in your group. Congratulations! I see, though, that the first quarter was not so good. What happened?"

The first quarter? That had been almost a year earlier! Adam had to think. What had happened a year ago? Oh, yes—he had an injured wing. He wasn't performing at his best.

"Of course," said Tony. "The injured wing. That would account for it. Well, it's too bad. If you had had a better first quarter, you would have won the prize for top producer. Instead you came in second. Better luck next year."

The first prize for top producer of the year was a cash bonus. There was no prize for second place. It reflected something that Daria liked to say at meetings: "In life, there's only first place. There is no second place!" Her speech was supposed to motivate the sales force, but it just depressed everyone. What was even more depressing was the obvious fact that the Minerva hive was nowhere near being number one, and the top leadership seemed not to care. They preached about being number one, but they didn't take any meaningful actions toward *becoming* number one.

As usual, because Adam was a cheerful bee, he pushed those thoughts out of his mind. He was fully loaded with high-quality nectar, and the sun was sinking toward the horizon. It was time to go back to the hive.

CHAPTER 4

AN UNEXPECTED DELAY

AS THE DAY GREW LONG, ADAM LEFT THE HYA-cinth garden and began the long flight home. He was proud of the fact that he had collected high-quality nectar and had exceeded his goal. It gave him a feeling of accomplishment, and he could retire for the night knowing that he had done a good job for his hive.

On a southward heading, he passed the tall building before turning east toward the center of the green valley. But as he flew with his heavy load, the sky began to darken. Heavy clouds were building in the west. With a feeling of anxiety, Adam hurried to stay ahead of the dark masses on the horizon. To be caught in a storm was not a good thing.

James had predicted a clear day, thought Adam. *Sure, it*

had started off as a nice day, but now things were very differ-ent. Adam thought that it was a miracle that James got any-thing done with that big messy pile of papers and charts that he kept in his cubicle. No one else could understand them. James was like an old-fashioned alchemist, one of those guys with a tall, pointed hat and mysterious instruments. He was busy all day, poring over charts and graphs, and he seemed like he was working hard. In fact, if you went to his cubicle and tried to talk to him, he'd always wave you away and say, "Can't you see I'm swamped with work? I can't possibly think of one more thing!" The problem for everyone else was that only James knew what he was doing. He gave his reports, and that was it. You couldn't ask him to explain because he'd get huffy, as if you were being nosy. He gave the appearance of being overworked, yet it wasn't clear to Adam what James did all day.

Adam glanced behind him. The big bank of dark clouds was gaining on him. *Must be a fast-moving sandstorm,* he thought. *I have to hurry!*

He came to the center of the valley and made his turn to go over the ridge. The old riverbed came into view, and Adam followed it toward the stand of scrubby trees. His wings were getting tired, but he thought he could make it back to the hive before the storm arrived.

As he was approaching the scrubby trees, the storm hit.

Suddenly, Adam was thrown upside down by a violent wind. The sand stung his eyes as he struggled to stay on course.

As he spun around, he saw landmarks flash in front of him: a familiar tree, the farmhouse. The powerful winds kept hurling him in different directions, and soon he was so confused that he didn't know which way was home.

The sky was now dark. As the wind howled, Adam knew that he had to find shelter soon; otherwise, he'd be blown too far off course. In front of him, he saw the farmhouse. *How is this possible? I already passed the farmhouse!*

He was flying in circles.

There—up ahead! The hive!

The familiar white, boxy shape gladdened Adam's heart. With his last bit of strength, he buzzed toward the entrance of the hive. It came closer—and then Adam's tiny legs landed on the welcome threshold of the little door.

He ran inside just as the wind and sand reached a new height of violence.

What a relief to be safe and sound!

As Adam caught his breath, he looked around. The place looked different. The rooms had been rearranged.

What was most alarming was that the bees he saw were not from the Minerva hive. They were strangers.

Adam had landed in the wrong hive!

With a feeling of horror, he turned to leave. It was better to risk the howling winds and sand than be in the wrong hive. He had heard stories from Daria and Tony about other hives. They were dark, brutal places where strangers were not treated kindly.

As Adam headed to the door, a voice called from behind him.

"Hey! Is that my old friend Adam?"

Adam was stunned. It was a voice he knew from the past. He turned. To his astonishment, standing in front of him was a bee he hadn't seen in months.

"Mike!" exclaimed Adam. "I thought you were dead!"

Mike came close and bowed. "Thankfully, my friend, nothing so dramatic has happened," he said cheerfully. "As you can see, I've never been in better health." He peered at Adam and his heavy load of nectar. "I see that you've done well in the garden today. I always knew you were a top performer! But your wings are full of sand. Surely you cannot be thinking of going back out into the storm."

"Well, I …" stammered Adam. "I mean, of course I cannot stay here."

"Why not?" replied Mike. "Come in. Make yourself comfortable. Here at the Venus hive, we enjoy having visitors—even from competing hives. I assume you're still at Queen Minerva's hive?"

"Yes," said Adam. "But how did you get here? Do you work here now? At the Minerva hive, we were told that you were lost on a mission. You went out one day and never came back. Everyone thought—well, you know. We thought the worst had happened."

"Fortunately, there was a happy ending," replied Mike. "Like you, I was blown off course and got lost. In desperation, I landed here. The bees here were so wonderful and welcoming that I have to confess that I never tried to go back to Queen Minerva. I hated to make everyone worry, but it really was for the best."

"Are they holding you here as a prisoner?" demanded Adam.

"Oh, no!" laughed Mike. "This is my new home. Come, I'll show you around."

Adam gratefully accepted. He was happy to see his old

friend and relieved that he didn't have to venture back out into the storm. His friends and colleagues at the hive would be worried, but when he returned after the storm, all would be well.

"I'll take you on a little tour of the place," said Mike. "Ah, here's the employee lounge. Perhaps you'd like some refreshments."

Adam was astonished—for two reasons. First, the employee lounge was clean and comfortable. Unlike the shabby employee lounge at the Minerva hive, this was a place that you'd actually want to go to. The second reason that Adam was astonished was because the employee lounge was actually full of employees!

"At Minerva hive," said Adam, "we have our employee lounge, but no one ever uses it. Everyone is afraid to be seen there because the managers will think you're lazy."

"My friend," said Mike, "you'll find that here at Venus hive, things are very different from what happens at Minerva hive. We're more relaxed. We enjoy both our work time and our break time. Right now, many of the workers are on their break."

"That's very nice," said Adam, "but let's be realistic. I'm sure that your productivity is not the same as Minerva's. How could it be?"

Mike shrugged. "I'm not going to answer that. I think you'll see for yourself."

With a confused heart, Adam followed his friend out of the employee lounge. He was both excited and a little bit fearful about what he was going to see.

They had not gone more than a few steps when another

bee who looked like a manager stopped Mike. Adam thought there might be trouble—after all, Mike had brought a visitor to the hive during working hours. At Minerva hive, that was unacceptable.

"Hello, Mike," said the bee. "I'm glad I ran into you. I wanted to tell you that your suggestion for how we can improve inventory tracking has been met with great enthusiasm. I think that we're going to implement your idea as soon as we get the upgraded software. I'll let you know."

"Thanks very much, Nancy," replied Mike. "Please allow me to introduce my friend Adam. He's from the Minerva hive and was caught in the storm."

Nancy and Adam exchanged pleasantries before Nancy said that she had to hurry off to an employee birthday party.

"That was your boss?" asked Adam. "She seems very nice."

"Actually, Nancy works in a different department," replied Mike. "I'm in sales, like you. She's in inventory control. She tracks the honey as it comes out of the factory."

"So why is she talking to *you*?" asked Adam.

Mike laughed. "My friend, there's a very good reason why I decided to stay here at the Venus hive. It wasn't just for the paycheck. I can make money anywhere. It was because of the culture here. It's very different from Minerva's. Here at Venus, everyone talks to everyone else. There are no barriers to communication. If I have an idea that I think will benefit the hive, I have no problem offering it to whoever might need it. In this case, I had an idea about inventory tracking. I thought it was a little crazy, but I thought, why not? The worst thing that could happen was that Nancy would say no."

"But aren't the managers worried that everyone will be putting their noses into everyone else's job?" asked Adam. "You know that at Minerva, we stick to our own jobs. They say it's more organized that way."

"I think that it comes down to trust," said Mike. "We trust each other. The managers know that the workers won't waste their time with frivolous nonsense. And the workers know that if they have an idea or a complaint, it will be listened to. My boss is not just someone who tells me what to do. She's more like a coach who helps me do the very best job that I can."

Mike checked his tiny smartwatch. "Good news! The weather report says the storm has passed. The sky is clear."

"You get that information directly—in real time?" asked Adam.

"Of course," replied Mike. "Don't tell me—is James still working at your hive?"

Adam nodded. The less said about poor befuddled James, the better.

"You've got a few minutes before sunset," said Mike. "The Minerva hive is a short flight from here. When you go outside, you'll immediately recognize where you are."

Grateful to his old friend for his hospitality, Adam headed for the door. Then he stopped and turned. "Thank you, Mike," he said, "By the way, if I were to bring someone from Minerva over here to see what I've seen, would that be all right?"

"No problem," replied Mike. "Of course there are certain areas of the hive that are off-limits to visitors, but I'd be glad to show a colleague from Minerva the public areas. I'll talk to my manager, and perhaps we can even arrange a quick meeting with the queen."

"Really?" replied Adam. "Queen Venus actually meets with regular workers?"

Mike smiled. "Like any chief executive, she's very busy; but she spends a good part of her day visiting areas of the hive. She likes to have personal contact with her employees."

"Thanks," said Adam. "I'll do my best to come back for a visit."

At the door, he saw that Mike was right: The storm had passed, and the late afternoon sun shone clear and cool.

As he flew back to Minerva, Adam thought about the amazing things he had seen.

How the employees seemed cheerful and happy to be at work.

How Mike and Nancy—bees from different departments—had exchanged ideas about how to improve the hive's operations.

How Mike had only to look at his smartwatch to get a real-time status report.

And above all, how the Venus hive seemed to be a happy place to work. It was no mystery, thought Adam as he flew, why a talented employee like Mike had chosen to stay there instead of returning to Minerva.

Up ahead, Adam saw the familiar white box of the Minerva hive. In less than a minute, he'd be back at work.

CHAPTER 5

TROUBLE WITH EVA

As the sun was nearing the horizon, Adam set down upon the smooth white threshold of the Minerva hive. All around him, his fellow drones and workers were returning from their missions. Many were heavily laden with nectar, but others had not fared so well. It was the end of a typical day, and all the salesbees were eager to get inside the safety of the hive, unload their goods, and settle down for the night.

Adam joined the line of salesbees who were headed to the receiving room. There, the nectar would be unloaded, inspected, weighed, and sorted into the appropriate storage areas.

The bee in charge of receiving nectar was the inventory manager, Eva. There's no polite way to say this, so I'll say it directly: all the traveling salesbees *hated* Eva. They dreaded every encounter with her. This was for two reasons.

First, she was just a plain old sourpuss. She constantly

complained about one ailment or another—her wings were stiff, or her knees were swollen, or her eyes were bothering her. One day, she announced that she had an infected antenna, and no one wanted to go near her for fear of catching whatever she had.

Now, there's no crime in having problems. We all have problems. But when you've got lots of bees trying to cooperate in the confined space of a beehive, no one wants to hear endless complaints about your personal health. What made it particularly unbearable was that whenever someone suggested that Eva see a doctor, she would snap, "Doctors! What do *they* know? I don't need a doctor. I need a *vacation*."

Well, don't we all want a vacation?

Being a tolerant bunch, Adam and the rest of the salesbees were willing to overlook Eva's personal quirks. What made them *really* dislike her was the second reason: She did not respect the salesbees. In fact, she seemed to take pleasure in being snide.

For example, in line in front of Adam was a novice bee named John. On that day, John had been sent out to work a rose garden that no one had ever visited before. It was virgin territory. Adam, being a veteran, knew that John had a tough job. You never sent a novice bee to a new territory unless you knew exactly what to expect. But Tony—the manager of drone activities—didn't know much of anything about the rose garden. He had simply told John to go there and come back with no less than five drops. It was a number he had produced by guesswork.

Now it was John's turn to face Eva.

"Okay, how much do you have?" said Eva in her most bored voice.

"Three drops," replied John. "But it's really good-quality—"

"Three?" Eva cut him off. "Your quota for today is five."

"Yes, but there was a sandstorm," said John.

"Not my problem," said Eva. "I'll have to mark you down as being short."

Adam thought that Eva took considerable pleasure in marking down John for being short. The more problems she could discover, the more it looked like she was doing a good job. Eva reported to Daria, who had the same mindset: she wanted to know who was not making their goals. But weirdly, Daria never said anything bad to Queen Minerva. It was better, said Daria, if the queen were not bothered by such details. Bad news would only upset her.

As a result, the Minerva hive was never able to get a clear picture of its honey business. The salesbees were constantly trying to fudge their numbers to please Eva. In return, Eva thought the salesbees were a bunch of lazy liars, and she never failed to criticize them. Meanwhile, Queen Minerva had no clue about the many challenges facing her team. No one told her anything negative, and she had no other way of getting accurate reports. Every department accused every other department of failing to meet goals, and Queen Minerva blithely issued memos that seemed to bees like Adam to be disconnected from reality.

Everyone at Minerva hive saw the problems—low morale,

antiquated equipment, lack of a team attitude, poor internal communications, and declining quality control—but no one did anything because no one knew how. They were all afraid of each other.

After Eva had thoroughly embarrassed John, it was Adam's turn to step up.

She peered at her old clipboard and said, "Let's see. You were sent to the western side of the green valley. To the hyacinths." She looked at the clock on the wall. "It's not a long trip. Why are you late?"

"What?" stammered Adam. "Late? But I've got a full ten drops! My quota was eight!"

Eva glanced at his load. "Yes—ten drops. Barely. I'd say more like nine and a half. Anyway, what do you want—a medal? I think that Tony sets the quotas much too low."

"That's crazy!" exclaimed Adam. His outburst was so un-characteristic that everyone in the room stopped and turned to look.

"Excuse me?" said Eva.

"It's not right!" said Adam. "I saw how you treated John, and he was trying to do his very best. And now you're giving me a hard time for *exceeding* my quota? That's just ridiculous!"

"Adam, do you want me to call Tony?" Eva reached for the rotary phone attached to the wall.

Adam took a deep breath. "Listen, Eva. I'm just trying to be fair. Can't we work together as a team? Believe me—this would never happen at the hive of Queen Venus!"

The room was stunned. For a moment, no one spoke.

Eva stared at Adam with an expression of disbelief. "And what do *you* know of the Venus hive?"

"Do you want to know?" asked Adam. "Okay, I'll tell you. They're beating us in every key performance indicator. Their sales are up while ours are down. The quality of their honey is improving while ours is declining. They're selling to the very same gourmet shops that we used to sell to."

"I've heard that Queen Venus is nothing more than a slave driver," sneered Eva.

"Not from what I saw," retorted Adam. "Their bees are happy at their work. Everyone gets along—even with their managers."

"And exactly how do you know this?" demanded Eva.

In the room, there was not a sound. Eva's question was a serious matter. It was unthinkable for a bee from one hive to visit another. It was something that you just didn't do.

"Because I was there today," replied Adam.

The bees gasped in astonishment.

"Silence!" Eva looked at Adam intently. "I don't believe you. You must have gotten hit on the head and become disoriented."

"I was disoriented, yes, but not from getting hit on the head. I lost my way in the sandstorm."

"I keep hearing talk about a sandstorm," said Eva. "But as you know, James predicted no sandstorm."

"Well, if you had gone outside this afternoon—" began Adam. Then he stopped. It was better to choose the battles you wanted to fight. "The point is that I was blown off course—and I landed at the Venus hive by mistake. I was there for about an hour, until the storm cleared and I flew here. I was lucky to get here before nightfall."

"And you were *inside* the Venus hive?" asked Eva.

"Yes."

Eva shook her head. "I'm sorry. It sounds like a tall tale. I'm putting you on report. You're grounded until further notice."

Ken, the malcontent, was in line behind Adam. "You're in trouble now," he sneered. "Couldn't have happened to a nicer guy. See what happens when you make waves? I knew you were headed for problems. You're going to be demoted to ordinary house drone!"

Adam was stunned. He didn't know what to do. Eva was ready to report him, and he knew that Tony would go along with whatever Eva did. That attitude was something that was particularly hurtful to Adam and to many of the other front-line workers. The managers wouldn't stick up for them. Adam remembered when he was sent to a flower garden beyond the farmhouse, but when he got there, the owner had cut all the flowers and sold them! That wasn't so bad—these things happen—but when he returned to the hive with no nectar, Tony didn't want to hear about what happened. It seemed obvious to Adam that someone had pulled an old report that listed the flower bed as viable when it wasn't, and Tony had used the out-dated report to make his assignments for the day. A mistake is a mistake. Everybody makes them.

Tony could have said, "Sorry, Adam, we goofed. We used a bad report. But thank you for drawing it to our attention. We'll make sure we update our maps with the new information so it won't happen again."

Tony *could* have said that, but he didn't. He just grumbled that Adam should have flown to another flower bed—and that to hit his quota, he'd have to make up the loss over the next week.

What am I, a worthless idiot? Adam thought. *I'm a perfectly reasonable bee who wants to contribute, but they act like I'm a criminal.*

And now it was the same thing all over again. In the Minerva hive, it was every bee for himself. No one stuck up for one other.

Everyone was trying to stab everyone else in the back. All that mattered was currying favor with the queen.

"Well, Adam?" insisted Eva. "Believe me, you can be replaced in a minute. There are a hundred bees who want your job. Are you going to get with the program?"

Adam snapped out of his thoughts. Every bee was staring at him. He looked at Eva. Surely there had to be a way to get through to her.

Suddenly, there came a fanfare from the corridor outside.

"The queen is coming!" came the call. "Make way for Queen Minerva!"

CHAPTER 6

ADAM FACES
THE QUEEN

IN THE RECEIVING ROOM, ALL THE BEES CAME TO attention.

Eva shot Adam a stern look that said, "You'd better behave yourself!"

One of the queen's attendants entered and announced, "Her Majesty Queen Minerva wishes to inspect the receiving area."

After the center of the room was cleared, attendants carried the queen in. It was an awe-inspiring moment because most of the ordinary workers had never seen the queen close up. Sitting on her portable throne, she was dressed in a regal robe with glittering jewels. Adam thought that the hive's many budget cuts certainly did not involve the queen!

As the queen surveyed the room, she pointed out various things to one of the executive committee members, who scribbled what she said onto a pad of paper.

We'll soon be getting more memos, thought Adam.

The queen talked briefly with Daria, the operations manager. None of what they said was audible to the attentive workers. It all seemed very private.

After a few minutes, the queen looked at the workers. Since entering the room, it was the first time she acknowledged their presence. Her expression was vaguely benign, like she was thinking of something else.

The workers stood stiffly at attention.

"Very good," said the queen in her perfect diction. "Please carry on."

At the signal that it was time to leave, her attendants knelt to pick up her throne and carry her away.

A wave of panic flooded over Adam. He was ruined—demoted to the rank of ordinary house drone. In the Minerva hive, it was business as usual: the same old intrigue, competition, and lack of trust. But Adam wanted the hive to be better! He was old enough to remember when it *was* better, when bees like Mike were still there, and all the bees took pride in their work, no matter how humble it was.

Just as the attendants were hoisting the heavy throne, Adam took a step forward. "Excuse me, Queen Minerva!" he said boldly. "I know where Mike is!"

All eyes turned to Adam.

The queen peered in his direction. "*What* did you say?" she asked.

"It was nothing," interjected Daria.

"Pay him no mind," added Eva.

"Are you *crazy*?" whispered Ken from behind Adam.

Daria motioned for the attendants to lift the queen's throne.

"No," ordered the queen. "Stop! I want to know what that bee said."

The room fell silent.

"Your majesty," said Adam, "I said that I know where Mike is."

"That's impossible," answered the queen. "Mike was lost on a mission. A tragedy. He's gone forever."

"That's right," added Daria. "He's gone."

"Forever," said Eva.

"You're in *deep trouble*!" whispered Ken from behind Adam.

"Step forward," ordered the queen. "What is your name?"

Adam complied. He stated his name.

"And you say that you know where Mike is?"

"Yes, ma'am," replied Adam.

"Where?" asked the queen.

Adam swallowed hard. It was the moment of truth.

"I saw him at the hive of Queen Venus," he said. "He works there now."

The bees in the room began talking excitedly to each other.

"Silence!" commanded Daria.

The room became silent.

"And when did you see him?" asked the queen.

"Your Majesty," answered Adam, "It was today. I was on a mission, and I got caught in a sandstorm. I got lost, and I accidently landed at the Venus hive. I stayed there until the storm was over. Mike showed me around the place."

"They didn't have you *arrested*?" demanded Daria.

"No," replied Adam. "Everyone was very nice. Mike told me that he got there the same way I did—he was blown off course. And, well, he liked it so much that he decided to stay there."

"This is impossible!" said Daria. "No one would ever do that!"

Another salesbee, perhaps emboldened by the example set by Adam, stepped forward. "Excuse me, Your Highness, but just last week when I was flying by the farmhouse, I passed a bee that I could swear was Mike. It was the strangest thing! I called to him, and he looked right at me. Then he kept going."

"No, no," said Eva. "You're obviously mistaken!"

Another salesbee stepped forward. "The same thing happened to me! I saw Mike flying over by the clover patch. I'd know him anywhere."

The queen raised her hand. Everyone stopped talking.

"Why didn't you say anything?" she asked the third bee.

"Say anything?" the bee replied. "Um … well … I didn't think I had the right to say anything. We had been told that Mike was gone. That was the company line. That was the story. I didn't want to get into trouble."

"This is outrageous!" said Daria. "If Mike is a traitor, then we need to deal with him! He must be a criminal!"

"What do you suggest?" asked the queen dryly. "We have him arrested? For what? Changing jobs?"

Daria didn't answer. She knew her outburst had been ridiculous. Mike had jumped ship for another hive. It was as simple as that.

The queen appeared lost in thought. She looked at Adam. "You say that Mike showed you around the Venus hive. What did you see?"

Adam hesitated. It was one thing to report that another bee had joined a competing hive. It was something else altogether to describe the operations of that competing hive in a way that would make the Minerva hive look bad. It might be considered extremely disloyal.

"You know that I care about this hive," said Adam.

"Yes," replied the queen.

"And you know that I have many friends here, and that I want nothing but the best for all of us here," he said.

"Yes, yes," interjected Daria. "We get all of that."

Adam noticed the stern look the queen gave Daria, and it gave him confidence. He took a deep breath, hoping the queen would not be angry. "Well, Mike told me why he joined the Venus hive."

"I'm sure they gave him a fat bonus check," said Daria.

"In fact, he specifically said that it was *not* for the money," replied Adam. "He stayed at the Venus hive because of the positive company culture. He feels appreciated there, and he has a reason to want to excel."

"Perhaps he simply feels more at home there," said the queen.

"With all due respect, Your Majesty, it's more than that. I saw for myself what he was talking about."

"What did you see?" asked the queen.

"An amazing lounge where employees enjoy spending their break time watching TV, playing ping-pong, making their own coffee and even much more. But the most significant thing I saw was that some of the managers were there too, mingling with the frontline workers."

"Sounds like a place with no discipline," said Daria.

Ignoring her comment, Adam continued to address the queen. "I saw an employee named Nancy come up to Mike and thank him for a suggestion that he had made. Nancy was from the control team, which is a different department from Mike, who is still a salesbee. She told him that they loved his idea, and to implement it they'd get the necessary software. And then Nancy had said she was going to a birthday party for one of the workers."

"Birthday party?" exclaimed Eva. "I've never heard of anything so absurd. I cannot imagine how it is the concern of any hive when a worker has a birthday. It's an entirely private matter."

"Oh, I don't know," said the queen. "I think it's a rather nice idea. We all like to have our birthdays recognized, don't we?"

Adam was encouraged by the queen's responses. Maybe, *just maybe*, she understood what he was talking about. He decided to take the biggest risk of all. "Your Majesty, that's not all. Mike said that the main reason he went to Venus was because of the way they do business. It's the team spirit. Everyone pulls for the other guy. No one cares what department you're in, or what your rank is. And what's more, the hive invests in the future. They have top-notch equipment. They're selling the kind of premium honey that we used to sell. They're adding capacity while we're cutting back. They're finding new markets while ours are drying up."

Queen Minerva gave Adam a hard look. The room was utterly silent.

"Now you've sealed your fate," whispered Ken from behind him.

Daria glared at Adam.

Eva fidgeted uncomfortably.

"And there's something else, Your Majesty," said Adam.

"Yes? What is it?"

"Mike invited me back. He said that he'd be happy to show me around their hive. Not to the private areas, of course—they have their production secrets just like we do—but he's willing to share some of their business concepts with us. He specifically mentioned something called 'employee engagement.' He says it's very important to their success."

"Employee engagement?" said Daria. "What's that? Does it have to do with bees getting married? Are they all engaged to each other?"

A ripple of laughter spread across the room. Even the queen showed a slight smile.

"No, no," insisted Adam. "I'm not sure what it is, but it's very powerful. Mike said that before they had employee engagement, the Venus hive was—well—" He looked at the queen. She gave him a little nod of encouragement. "It was," he continued bravely, "sort of like how we are right now. I mean, not exactly operating at our very best. Lots of problems. No offense to Your Majesty, of course."

The room was silent. All the bees wondered how the queen would respond.

For several long seconds, the queen said nothing. Then she said, "Here at the Minerva hive, we take great pride in our work. We have a long, distinguished tradition of quality and excellence. But you, Adam, are of the opinion that things could be better?"

"Go ahead," whispered Ken from behind him. "Hang yourself!"

"Yes," said Adam. "And I believe that I'm not the only one, Your Majesty."

There was another long pause as the queen seemed to be thinking.

"As a matter of fact," she said at length, "I share your desire for improvement. It seems to me that we've gotten ourselves in a bit of a rut recently. I too remember when we were at the top of our industry. And while it's nice to be self-sufficient and to think that all the answers you need are right in your own hive, sometimes you have to swallow your pride and get some outside help. I remember the words of our esteemed grandfather, the founder of this hive. He said that you should always surround yourself with people who are smarter than you. You should learn from them."

At these words, Eva and Daria and the other senior bees shuffled their feet uncomfortably.

"Tell me," continued Queen Minerva, "does Mike still have warm feelings about his time here?"

"Oh, yes," replied Adam. "He told me that his decision was nothing personal. It was just business. He had to do what was best for his career."

"Of course," said the queen. "All right. Here is my decision. I hereby authorize you to return to the hive of Queen Venus. You will leave at daybreak. Stay as long as necessary. Your task is to learn all that you can about this concept of employee engagement. Find out how it helps the Venus hive and if it can help us."

Adam could hardly believe his ears. "Thank you, Your Majesty!" he exclaimed.

"And one more thing," said the queen. "I want another bee to accompany you, someone who will provide a second viewpoint."

"I have someone in mind," said Adam.

"Who?"

"Your Majesty, I think it would be a good idea if a bee from another department came—someone not in sales. In your nursery there is a bee named Susan. I think she'd be a good choice."

The queen turned to the manager of the nursery. "You have someone named Susan working for you?"

"Yes, ma'am," replied the manager. "She has a good employment record with us."

After thinking for a moment, the queen said to Adam, "All right, it is agreed. You shall both go."

Then she addressed the nursery manager. "Give Susan the necessary time off, with pay." With those words, the queen signaled for her throne to be lifted. Her attendants hoisted her into the air. Then she turned to Adam. "One more thing," she said. "When you return, you will report to me directly." She turned to Daria, who had trouble hiding her bitterness. "Please ensure that Adam is escorted to me the moment he returns."

"Yes, ma'am," said Daria.

The queen was carried out of the room.

"I knew you'd do it!" Ken slapped Adam on the back. "Say, listen, when you see the queen, put in a good word for me, your old friend Ken, won't you?"

Adam sighed. *Some bees never change.* "Listen, Ken, I have to go. I need to get some sleep." With his head full of confused but exhilarating thoughts, Adam hurried back to his cubicle.

CHAPTER 7

VISITING THE HIVE OF QUEEN VENUS

THE NEXT MORNING WAS CLEAR AND COOL. Adam met Susan at the front door, and they took off for the flight to the Venus hive.

"I was surprised when they told me that I had been chosen for this mission," said Susan as they buzzed over the green fields.

"I thought it was important to get the perspective of two different departments," said Adam. "I spend a lot of time outside the hive. I know a lot about sales and inventory. You work in the nursery."

"Yes," said Susan. "I don't leave the hive very often. I'm glad you're here to navigate. I'd surely get lost! But I think that I have a good understanding of how the hive works on a day-to-day basis. I see all the things that go on. I see all the competition and backstabbing. Believe me, sometimes it seems more like a shark tank than a beehive!"

"Maybe we can help change that," said Adam. "I'll bet this thing called employee engagement will help us. I'm not sure what it is, but it sounds good."

In a few minutes, they arrived at the Venus hive. After landing by the door, they looked at each other.

"Ready?" said Adam.

"Ready as I'll ever be!" replied Susan.

Once inside, they asked a few bees if Mike were available. They didn't have to wait long before he appeared.

"Susan!" he exclaimed. "How wonderful to see you again. It's been a long time. And, of course, you too, Adam. Welcome to the hive of Queen Venus."

"We thank you for agreeing to see us," said Susan.

"It's our pleasure," replied Mike. "I spoke to my manager about your visit. Andrew has allowed me to show you around. In fact, Queen Venus herself will be giving us a few minutes of her time later on. She's got a very busy schedule, but she wanted to meet you."

"We're looking forward to it," said Adam. "I'm sure you know why we're here. When I dropped in yesterday—quite by accident—you mentioned something about employee engagement and how wonderful it was. We hope you can tell us more about it."

"That's the plan!" said Mike. "Our first stop will be the

employee lounge. You can hang out there for a while and talk to bees from the various departments. The employee lounge is right next to the day-care center. There's always a lot of activity there."

Mike led the way to the employee lounge.

"Everyone here seems so cheerful," whispered Susan as they made their way along the crowded corridor. "And the place is so clean. Not a speck of dirt anywhere."

"It seems weird at first, doesn't it?" replied Adam. "But I could get used to it. I mean, if we had it back at the Minerva hive."

They entered the spacious employee lounge, where bees were sitting at tables or playing ping-pong—which, since bees can play with a paddle in each tiny hand, is a very fast-paced game.

Adam also noticed a lot of activity at the foosball tables. "Those players look very serious," he said to Mike.

"Today we play the finals of the interdepartmental foosball tournament, which everyone's looking forward to," Mike replied. "Ah, come this way!" He ushered Adam and Susan to a table where a bee was drinking a latte. "I asked our director of human resources if he would spend a few minutes with you today. Please allow me to introduce Robert."

After appropriate greetings, Susan, Adam, and Robert sat down. Mike went to get them coffees from the machine.

"Thanks for agreeing to see us," said Adam. "We're hoping to learn about employee engagement. It's not something that we know much about at our hive. I suppose you could say that we're a little bit behind the times."

"I understand," said Robert. "Here's how we see it. There are two kinds of hives. The old-fashioned kind is where you have an authority figure at the top—either one person or an executive committee—from whom all direction flows. The leader collects business information, makes decisions, and issues directions to subordinates. The subordinates carry out the orders. Under such a system, subordinates are encouraged to compete with one another for rewards such as promotions or bonuses. While some people believe this vertical or top-down system is efficient, in reality, it is deeply flawed. There is no free flow of information. Employees have no reason to be loyal. It's hard to respond to changing market conditions because everyone has to wait around for the top executive to make every decision.

Departments are *siloed*, which is just what it sounds like—everyone is in his or her own little tube, and the tubes only lead up to the bosses, not to each other."

"To be honest," said Susan, "what you're describing sounds a lot like the Minerva hive."

"And many more hives as well," said Robert. "The other type of organization is one that's structured more like a team. The CEO is the coach. While you still have a hierarchy with ranks and job descriptions, the relationships between the members of the team are very different. Bees are encouraged to exchange ideas, even if they seem far-fetched. If someone makes a mistake, his or her boss will help the worker figure out how to avoid making the same mistake again."

"Like a coach of a sports team," said Adam.

"Exactly," said Robert. "This is why it's called *employee engagement*. The employees are part of the fabric of the operation. They care about the organization. They are empowered to represent the organization. This is in contrast to employees who are not engaged. These unfortunate bees do what they're told to do, take their paychecks, and then go home. The hive doesn't matter to them because they don't matter to the hive."

"But you must have annual performance reviews—don't you?" asked Susan.

"While it's true that we need to keep a formal file on every bee," replied Robert, "in our culture of coaching, praise and criticism are delivered immediately. Think about it—if a team member does something wonderful, why on earth would you wait six months to thank them? And if they make a mistake, wouldn't you want to tell them right away? Here at the Venus hive, at the end of the day we want every bee to feel they've been treated fairly and with respect. We want transparency—no games, no secrets."

"You must award performance bonuses," said Adam.

"Commissioned salesbees get bonuses, but that's part of their pay structure," replied Robert. "For most of us, we have a profit sharing program. Every year, our employees receive a share of the hive's profits. It gives everyone an incentive to work together as a team."

"I think that the Minerva hive is full of disengaged bees," Susan said to Adam.

"As you can see here," said Robert, "It's possible to do things in a very different way."

Chapter 8

New Ideas

A BEE PASSED THE TABLE, AND ROBERT TURNED TO her. "Say, Sara, do you have a minute? There are some friends here I'd like you to meet."

With a smile, she stopped. "Sure! I'd be happy to chat for a few minutes."

After introductions were made, Susan said, "Robert told us that you're in the marketing department and that you're in charge of social media. How does that work? What do you do?"

Sara seemed puzzled by the question.

"What my colleague didn't tell you," said Adam, "Is that at our hive, we don't use social media. Of course, as individuals we do, but we do it on our own time. The hive doesn't have any social media engagement."

"Oh, I see," replied Sara in the tone that you use when

you're feeling sorry for someone who has suffered a misfortune. "Here's the basic idea. An increasing number of our customers are turning to the Internet to find information about our business and our products. Long-established businesses like ours must find ways to reach out to this new generation of social media-obsessed shoppers. Because of our customers, a robust online presence has become important to our success."

"Sometimes when I'm out in the field," said Adam, "another bee will ask me for our website address. I don't even know what it is. As far as I know, the only reason we even have a website is to *sell* to people. We don't, like, *talk* to them or anything."

"I see," said Sara. "But surely you understand that a website—and your social media program—can be like a window into your company. You can see your customers, and they can see you."

"At the Minerva hive," said Susan, "customers are not encouraged to see what's inside!"

"Which is why we never know what our customers are thinking or what they want," added Adam.

"I understand," said Sara. "Here at the Venus hive, we believe that communication with our customers is very important. I'll give you an example. Last year, we made a big batch of orange honey. We got the flavoring from that orange grove in the eastern end of the green valley. I'm sure you know the place. Anyway, we offered this new orange honey to our customers. We thought it was going to be a big seller. As soon as we put it on the shelves, our Facebook page started to get comments. To our surprise, most of the comments were negative! Everyone said that the honey was too bitter. People even took it back to the store. I went online and asked our customers to tell me more. They all said that they assumed it was going to be *sweet* orange honey. As it turns out, the oranges in the grove at the eastern end of the green valley are Seville oranges, which are not very sweet. Based on what our customers were telling us, we realized that we had simply marketed the orange honey improperly. I told the product managers that they should repackage the honey and call it Seville orange honey. If they did this, the consumers would know what to expect. This was done right away. We sold it as Seville orange honey, and suddenly everyone liked it! This was because they knew what to expect."

"I remember the Minerva hive trying those same orange blossoms," Adam quietly said to Susan. "It was a disaster. The honey didn't sell, and no one knew why!"

"So you're saying," Susan said, "that after the product was launched, you engaged your customers and solicited their feedback. And then you took their opinions and realized the company needed to make a change. You went to the product manager and told him what you had learned. The product manager ordered the change to be made, and the product became successful."

"Yes, that's pretty much exactly what happened."

"It sounds like *employee* engagement is also *customer* engagement," said Adam.

"Sure," said Robert. "The two go hand in hand. You can't have one without the other."

"How about the product manager who initially approved the marketing of the orange honey?" asked Susan. "Did he or she get fired?"

"Fired?" said Robert. "Oh, no. It was obvious that there had been a series of mistakes all along the process of development and production. Lots of bees failed to notice the problem. No one got fired. To make sure it doesn't happen again, we developed a protocol for correctly identifying the nectar that comes into the hive and making sure that every batch of honey has an unbroken pedigree. We learned from our mistake."

"But how do you correct an employee who truly doesn't understand what he or she needs to do?" asked Susan.

"The first rule is that you do it privately," said Robert. "Have a witness present if necessary, but be respectful and honest. Make it very clear what you expect. Offer to get him or her training if necessary. Be a coach, not a boss. But if—like a coach—you need to cut bees from the team, do it quickly and with dignity. Thank them for their service, and send them on their way. Keeping a malcontent on the job is not fair to the other employees. Keeping someone like that is seen as rewarding poor performance with continued employment."

"I have another question about your social media program," said Susan. "Is it expensive?"

"One of the advantages of social media is the low cost," replied Sara. "Rather than spending millions of dollars for a World Cup TV ad, for example, we've learned to generate interest by creating viral content and encouraging shares and likes. Once a product becomes the one everyone is talking about, customers want to learn more, and they gravitate toward it. Or, in the case of the orange honey, they criticize it. But that's okay because we learn from the criticism."

"The best part about social media marketing is that it can be deployed without spending millions," added Robert. "If a company handles it on their own, like we do, it costs nothing but the time of the person doing the updates."

"What's important," added Sara, "is that the CEO—in our case, Queen Venus—realizes the value of social media in driving decisions. We ask ourselves about which posts on Facebook received the most likes. We ask ourselves how many customer complaints came through Twitter last month. The insight we develop come from gathering statistics on that information, and we use it to gain an edge over the competition."

"And by the way," added Robert, "Queen Venus has her own Twitter account. She's directly engaged with our customers!"

Sara glanced at her phone. "I hope you'll excuse me. I have a stand-up meeting now. It was a pleasure to meet you both!"

"A stand-up meeting?" asked Adam as Sara left the table.

"Yes," said Robert. "These daily meetings usually last ten minutes. They're held standing up to encourage people to keep the meeting short and on topic. Typically, there are only three questions to ask and answer in the daily stand-up: What did I accomplish yesterday? What will I do today? And what obstacles are impeding my progress? All of the members of a given team are encouraged to attend, but if some of the team members are not present, the meetings still take place. These short meetings encourage closer working relationships and result in a better exchange of knowledge from one bee to another. Team members take turns speaking, and sometimes they'll even pass a token; only the person holding the token is allowed to speak."

"It sounds like a very efficient way to get everyone on the same page," said Susan.

"Absolutely," agreed Robert. "Here at Venus hive, we strive to make sure everyone has the information he or she needs to do the job—and that the information is accurate and timely. We use networked computer dashboards to disseminate real-time data to everyone who needs it."

"Even the weather guy?" asked Adam. He was thinking about poor James, with his stacks of paper printouts.

"*Especially* the weather guy," said Robert. "He has a complete digital weather station. It was expensive to set up, but it's paid for itself many times over. Our weather guy has the authority to cancel a flight if he sees bad weather coming."

"Really?" said Adam. "At Minerva hive, only the operations manager can cancel a flight. And if she's in a meeting, you can't talk to her."

CHAPTER 9

MOVING THE HIVE FORWARD

MIKE, WHO HAD LEFT THE TABLE FOR A FEW MIN-
utes, came back. "Our sales team is having lunch with our supervisor," he said. "Why don't you come over and sit in?"

Robert, Adam, and Susan made their way to a table on the
other side of the employee lounge, where food was served. The
group of six bees made room for the visitors.

"Welcome," said the supervisor of sales. "My name is
Andrew. To celebrate the fact that we surpassed our goal for
this week, I'm buying everyone lunch!"

The five other bees smiled and thanked him.

"Yes, it was a good team effort," continued Andrew.
"Charles, I want to thank you for covering for Paula when she

was out sick one day. Because you put in the extra hours, we stayed on track."

Charles—an older bee at the end of the table—smiled and said, "No problem. You guys covered for me when I had my accident and was out for a week. It was the least I could do."

Adam was astounded by what he saw. At the Minerva hive, he had never been invited to lunch by Tony or any other supervisor. Unlike the collaborative culture in the hive of Queen Venus, his working environment was characterized by competition and intrigue. The sales totals for each member of his group were posted at the end of each month. The top salesbee got a bonus. Everybody else got only his or her expected commission. And if you were near the bottom of the list, you received a warning.

Tony never thanked Adam—or any other salesbee—for a job well done. Adam received comments only in January during his annual performance review. For eleven months per year, he toiled with very little feedback about his performance. Oh, sure, if he showed up late or was short on his quota, Tony or Eva would reprimand him. But he learned nothing from their lectures. He did not need to be told he was late—he already knew that! When he was late returning to the hive one day, Tony yelled at him. Tony wasn't interested in the reason Adam was behind schedule; he just wanted to exert his authority. In fact, the reason that Adam was late returning from his mission was because Tony had given him an outdated map! The old map showed a flower bed that had been replanted with flowers that bloomed later in the season. When Adam arrived, he found nothing but immature buds. On his own, he had discovered another flower bed a mile away. He made his quota, but he had been late returning to the hive.

It would have been so *normal*, so *rational*, for Tony to ask Adam why he was late. Adam would have told him about the outdated map. Tony would have said, "Oh, I'm terribly sorry. Thank you for this valuable information. We'll make sure that the map is updated so that the next bee doesn't get sent to that garden when the flowers aren't blooming." Yes, that would have been the logical response.

But at the Minerva hive, interactions between managers and workers weren't based on a rational approach to improvement. It was something else. The more he thought about it, the more he realized that the pervasive culture at the Minerva hive was one of *mistrust*. No one trusted anybody else.

Eva did not trust that the salesbees were providing an honest count of their quotas.

Daria did not trust the employees enough to have something as simple as a nice employee lounge. And she did not trust that the queen was capable of hearing bad news.

Tony did not trust what his salesbees told him about their experiences in the field.

Ken didn't trust *anybody*.

And, yes, Adam had to admit that he never trusted the weather reports issued by James. They were completely useless.

It was strange, thought Adam, that the first sign of trust he had experienced at the hive was when the queen asked him to go on this mission! She had been opposed in her decision by her executive team. They were not interested in what a lowly salesbee and a girl from the nursery could discover about the company culture at a competing hive. They probably thought Adam and Susan just wanted to goof off for a day or two.

Yet Queen Minerva had entrusted him and Susan with this important task. She could have asked Daria or one of the other executives to go, but she didn't.

Perhaps the queen didn't trust her own executive team.

After the lunch meeting had broken up, Robert took Adam and Susan to the nursery. It also served as an employee day care center where bees with families could bring their young children to be cared for during the workday.

"Imagine," said Susan, "the children of the workers mingling with the children of the queen! That would never happen at the Minerva hive."

"Funny thing," said Adam. "As I recall, it was Daria who made that rule. She said the queen was against all the children being put together. But I wonder if the queen ever actually said that—or whether it was invented by Daria."

As they were talking in the nursery, a bee came in to drop off her child. Before she left to go back to work, Robert asked her to come over.

"This is Rachel," he said. "She works in the honey-production department."

"We're pleased to meet you," said Adam. "We were talking

with Sara about the product launch for the orange honey, and how you quickly made changes based on customer feedback. How did that affect you?"

Rachel laughed. "Well, I still have my job, which is a good thing! But seriously, that's a very good example of how we try to practice *kaizen*, or continuous improvement. Anyone in the production area can offer a suggestion for an improvement or even halt production if they see something wrong. When Sara brought us the information about how our customers disliked the new orange honey, the manager on duty immediately shut down the line. After we got more information, we realized that we needed new labels for the honey jars. The marketing team made up the new labels—the ones that now say 'Seville Orange Honey'—and we quickly relabeled the existing jars. In less than a day, we were back on track. What could have been a major disaster was fortunately only a minor setback."

"Because the employees care about their products and the company, the outcome was good," said Susan.

"Definitely," said Rachel. "Each one of us—from the queen herself to the bees who clean the hive—is important to our success. We all have our jobs to do, but we're always looking out for each other."

Adam thought for a moment. "That sounds good, but surely you have standards that you expect everyone to meet? You must have goals that have to be reached. That takes disciplined effort."

"Absolutely," said Rachel. "In the production department,

we have goals. We call them SMART goals. SMART is an acronym that stands for specific, measurable, achievable, relevant, and time-bound."

"That sounds sensible," said Susan. "Too often at our hive, our goals seem arbitrary and unrealistic. The executive team sets goals for the quarter, but after a few weeks, we realize that we need to adjust them. But they always stay the same. Can you describe how SMART goals work?"

"Sure," said Rachel. "I'll go through them one by one. "*Specific* means that you clearly define what you expect the employee to do or deliver. Avoid generalities. For example, in the production department, our goal is for our honey to be 99.9 percent pure. For an agricultural product, that's pretty high. We sell only Grade A—nothing less.

"*Measurable* means that we know how we measure success. It's not a matter of opinion. If our goal is to produce a thousand jars of clover honey in a week, that's our goal. Everyone knows it. We also strive to have only one broken or defective jar per thousand produced—even if it's something as minor as a label that's put on crooked. Every production line has a quality-control team checking every jar. If they find a defect, they'll stop the line to make sure the problem is corrected.

"*Achievable* means that accomplishing the goal is within the hive's realm of authority and capabilities. We ask if the hive can successfully complete a goal with the skills, resources, and time available to us. Are there factors beyond our control that need to be considered? For example, when the farmer suddenly dug up his flower beds, we had to scramble to adjust our production goals. We increased the amount of clover honey to compensate for the loss of the flowers.

"*Relevant* means that the goal *should be met* and *can be met*. A goal may be theoretically achievable but not meaningful to long-term success. We try to link every goal to a higher-level departmental or organizational goal and ensure that every employee understands how his or her actions contribute to the attainment of the higher-level goal. This gives them a context for their work."

"I see what you mean about engaging the employees with their goals," said Susan. "Sometimes at our hive, we have goals assigned to us and we have no idea what they mean. Everything just seems so random. All we hear is, 'Do this, do that.' We don't get the big picture."

Rachel nodded. "It's depressing to do a job and not have any sense of how your product or service helps people to live better lives! The essence of employee engagement is that your work has meaning and that you know how you're contributing to the success of the hive.

"The last part of a SMART goal is that it's *time-bound*," she continued. While you need to set quantitative goals—like a thousand jars of honey—the time factor is equally important. Our customers expect our products to be delivered on time. What if someone wants a special jar of honey for a holiday and we don't deliver it until *after* the holiday? We'd have a very unhappy customer. Their holiday dinner might have been ruined. We're in the business of making people happy, and if we don't, we've failed."

Adam frowned. "I understand. Sadly, at our hive, the goal is to shove the product out the door. No one cares about quality or customer service."

"The reason they don't care," added Susan, "is because the workers don't trust the managers, and the managers don't trust the workers. Everyone is in it for himself or herself."

"Yes, trust is the foundation," said Rachel. "Oh, look at the time! I have to get back to my office. It was nice to meet you both, and I wish you good luck."

After their visit to the nursery, before it was time to say good-bye there was one more bee to meet.

Robert escorted Adam and Susan to the office of Queen Venus. Unlike Queen Minerva's sumptuous chambers, Queen Venus's office looked like a regular office. The door wasn't even closed—anyone could just walk in!

Hmm, thought Adam. *Once again, it's all about trust. The queen trusts her subordinates not to waste her time with trivial issues that they could solve themselves.*

Queen Venus received them graciously. "I hope you've had a pleasant and productive visit," she said. "Here at the Venus hive, we make employee engagement part of our company culture. It's something we do every day. And I truly believe that it has led to our success."

"Queen Venus," asked Susan, "what do you think is the most important key to achieving employee engagement?"

"It's in hiring the right people," she answered. "I can train anyone to make good honey. But I cannot train someone to be honest, to be imaginative, or to be trustworthy. Those are qualities that you need to bring to the job yourself."

CHAPTER 10

OPPORTUNITY AT THE MINERVA HIVE

WITH A SENSE OF EXCITEMENT, ADAM AND SUSAN waved good-bye to their friends at the hive of Queen Venus and headed for home. The sun was still high in the sky, and the farm buzzed with activity. As they flew over the green meadows, they thought about all the things they had seen and talked about.

They especially thought about how in the Venus hive, all of the bees trusted each other. It seemed to Adam and Susan that trust and openness were the keys to employee engagement and sustained success.

After landing at the Minerva hive, they were met by Daria who—grudgingly, it seemed—escorted them to the private office of the queen.

The difference between the offices of Queen Venus and Queen Minerva was dramatic. Where the office of Queen Venus had been functional and elegant, the office of Queen Minerva was ostentatious and even a bit gaudy. It was designed to *look* impressive, but Adam wondered how anything got done in such a cluttered environment.

The queen was behind her big gold-trimmed desk. "Please— sit down," she said.

Adam and Susan took their seats facing her.

A group of bees entered the room.

"Ah, the executive committee is here," said the queen. "Good. Now we can begin."

Daria went to close the door.

"Excuse me, Daria," said the queen. "I think we'll just leave the door open. Thank you."

With a little shrug, Daria sat down.

"Now then," said the queen. "Adam and Susan, please tell us everything you saw. Don't leave out a single detail."

Adam and Susan glanced at each other. Now was the moment of truth. They each took a deep breath and, taking turns, told the story of their visit to the Venus hive.

They revealed to the queen and the executive committee how the Venus hive had a culture of respect, where everyone's contribution was valued; and when problems arose they were handled quickly and privately. The workers trusted their managers, and their trust was reciprocated. The hive had a team attitude, where each bee did his or her part to reach a common goal. And, as Queen Venus had told them, the foundation of an engaged culture lay in hiring the right bees—the team players who were a good fit.

Adam and Susan hinted—but politely did not say directly—that the culture of the hive started at the very top and worked its way through the ranks. If the queen were committed to a policy of employee engagement, the company's culture would follow along.

As they told their story, Queen Minerva nodded thoughtfully. Occasionally she would ask them to repeat something or clarify a detail. Then she would ask them to continue.

Meanwhile, her private secretaries busily wrote down every word.

All around them, Adam and Susan were aware of subdued murmuring from the bees on the executive committee. No one dared speak while the queen was listening to Adam and Susan, but the committee members could not help themselves.

"That's *crazy*," one of them whispered.

"I think it sounds good," said another.

"It will *never* work here," murmured a third.

"We should try it," said a fourth.

At one point, the queen held up her hand. "You talked about computer-networked dashboards; how do they help create employee engagement?"

"Look at it this way," said Adam. "Imagine if James, the weatherbee, had a computer that showed him all the weather reports instantly. He would become much more effective at his job. But that's just a technology upgrade. Now imagine if *your* computer on *your* desk showed the exact same weather report that James was looking at. And the computer on Tony's desk showed it too. Maybe not in the same detail, but a simplified version. Now every member of the team would be looking at the same information. If James saw bad weather coming, he could send you an email or an alert that said, 'Please pay attention to this report.' You could see it instantly and decide what to do."

"It sounds like employee engagement will help me, too," said the queen. "I'd know more about what was going on in the hive, and I'd spend less time attending to every detail." The queen thought for a moment and looked at the assembled group. "I am not unaware that this hive has suffered a decline in our business. We've been doing the same thing for much too long. Other hives are making progress while we stay at the same level. Unfortunately, in business, if you stay at the same level, others overtake you. You cannot become complacent. I would be happier, and I'm sure the members of this hive would be happier, if we took more of a team approach. If we made an effort to bring out the very best in each other, rather than seeking to uncover the worst, we'd be more productive."

One of the executive committee bees raised his hand. "Your Majesty, I understand what you're saying, but I'm concerned about discipline. Won't such an open company culture lead to chaos and disrespect for authority?"

The queen shook her head. "Those who have the authority to hire and fire will still have that authority, won't they? Then why should they be afraid? If a bee is not a good fit for our hive, and we try to make it work for him or her but it doesn't work, then we must tell that bee to find a more appropriate place of employment. But if you're asking whether it takes more energy to lead thoughtfully and with empathy, then you're right—it does. The lazy way is to issue memos or wave your hand and say, 'Do this, do that.' But bees are not robots, and you must be willing to invest in your bees. Not just with money, but with your heart, too."

"Excuse me, Your Majesty," said another member of the

executive team, "but many of our bees have been with us their entire lives. They have an ingrained way of doing things."

"Yes, they have a sense of tradition," said another bee. "Change is not viewed favorably. No one wants to think that he or she will lose position or power."

The queen smiled. "I think that employee engagement is about the fundamental perception we have of each other. Do we see each other as competitors and enemies? Do the managers see their subordinates as untrustworthy and lazy? Do the workers see us—their bosses—as tyrants? In today's economy, how can such an organization survive? But to your point, if we choose to embrace employee engagement, some of our senior members may be faced with a new set of expectations. Many will bend. A few will refuse and remain rigid. Over time, those who remain rigid will grow increasingly unhappy. They may have to find a more suitable situation elsewhere." The queen glanced at an ornate clock on the wall. "I see it is time for my inspection of the production facilities. I thank you all for coming here. I will consider what we've discussed today and give you my decision first thing tomorrow."

The bees left the queen's office and returned to their stations.

"What do you think will happen?" asked Susan as she and Adam made their way along the corridor.

"Your guess is as good as mine!" replied Adam. "I think that the queen understands the concept of employee engagement and sees the benefits. But there are many others who like things just the way they are. They may resist."

"If change doesn't come," said Susan, "there will be many more bees like Mike who will seek a better life at another hive."

Adam stopped and looked at Susan. "I think that we can both agree that the future will be interesting!"

They parted ways and looked forward to the next morning and the queen's decision.

THE OWNER AND THE CONSULTANT

AFTER READING *A TALE OF TWO BEEHIVES* TO THE very last page, the owner of the company closed the book. He turned to the consultant.

"That was a terrific story!" he said. "But tell me—what happens in the end? I'm in suspense! Did Queen Minerva keep things the way they'd always been, or did she change the culture of her hive to promote employee engagement?"

The consultant smiled. "I don't know. It could have gone either way, couldn't it? Queen Minerva was shown a new path, and she could have either refused to follow it or boldly taken action." The consultant leaned forward and looked the business owner in the eye. "Tell me—what would *you* advise Queen Minerva to do?"

"I'd tell her to wake up and accept reality," replied the business owner. "Her hive faced many big problems. It was no longer competitive, and its internal systems were outdated and cumbersome. Employees didn't trust each other and didn't work as a team. The departments were siloed and didn't exchange information and ideas.

"Meanwhile, at the Venus hive the queen saw herself less like a director and more like a coach. Her job was to bring out the very best in all of her employees. She knew that in today's competitive business environment, no business owner can afford to overlook the talents and abilities of any employee. A well-coordinated team whose activities are based on a foundation of respect and empowerment will outperform a competitor whose organization clings to the old top-down model where the big boss gives orders and everyone blindly follows them."

"So you would say that in addition to Queen Venus being a nice person who is pleasant to work with, there are sound business reasons for her management choices?" asked the consultant.

"Absolutely," replied the business owner. "Queen Venus is no dummy! She knows that a culture of employee engagement makes her business *more* competitive and *more* profitable. Therefore, she empowers her executive team members, since she realizes that setting the organizational culture starts from the top. It's true that employee engagement may incur some higher short-term costs. Queen Venus invested in the employee lounge, and I'm sure her employee benefits—things like longer maternity leave and more extensive employee training programs—are expenses. But these investments bring a substantial return! Her employee productivity and loyalty are high, and she has low employee turnover. Her employees are eager to offer new ideas because they know they'll be listened to."

"Do you think Queen Venus has lower standards for her employees than Queen Minerva?" asked the consultant. "Is she just a softy?"

"No," replied the business owner. "In fact, I'm sure she holds her employees to a *higher* standard of excellence. There is a saying I've heard—"Hire slow, fire fast." This means that you're careful whom you bring onboard. You need to make sure that everyone you hire is a good fit for your company. But if a person just doesn't understand and can't be a good team player, you need to separate them quickly. Don't let them drag everyone else down. And always remember, cleaning up the stairs always starts from the top."

"You're right," replied the consultant. "If you want to be on a winning team, then Queen Venus wants you. Her employees work hard and take great pride in what they do. They go home knowing that they're part of an organization that has meaning and is helping their customers lead better, happier lives."

"It doesn't get any better than that!" said the business owner.

"What are you going to do?" asked the consultant.

"I'm going to order a copy of *A Tale of Two Beehives* for each member of my senior staff," said the business owner. "Then we're going to start making some changes."

The consultant smiled. "Good idea!"

NOTES

NOTES

NOTES

NOTES

NOTES

NOTES

NOTES

NOTES

NOTES

NOTES

A Piece of Peace

The quest for wisdom is an ageless pursuit that rewards the seeker with a lifetime of knowledge, satisfaction, and personal success. These are riches that never lose value with the passing of time.

In the ancient tradition of handing down wisdom through the art of storytelling, author Sharoq Almalki has curated a collection of 110 fables and allegories, each paired with a moral explanation. Rich with advice for personal and professional success, they both entertain and guide the reader toward developing strength, kindness, sincerity, honesty, integrity, and many other characteristics of the wise.

Learn how to ask for help and work with a team, rather than trying to accomplish your goals alone. Understand how to maintain and utilize your creativity instead of letting technology think for you. Believe in yourself, and respect failure without fearing it. Studying these stories and their lessons will infuse your work with soul, spirit, and passion. You'll begin to stand out from the workforce as a productive and successful employee who is fun to work with and be around.

Read through, and learn from, *A Piece of Peace,* and, in the end, you may become known for your wisdom, too!

ISBN: 978-1500752262

To learn more, visit:
www.sharoqalmalki.com

www.ingramcontent.com/pod-product-compliance
Lightning Source LLC
Chambersburg PA
CBHW022057170526
45157CB00004B/1381